AF428397

ECOSYSTEM FACTS THAT YOU SHOULD KNOW

THE FRESH AND SALTWATER

EDITION

Nature Picture Books | Children's Nature Books

Have you ever wondered how plants and animals survive in our waters? Because of the Earth's ecosystem, each organism works together, as well as working with the sun and the water to make this possible. In this book, you will be learning about the marine and freshwater ecosystems.

Landscape in Donana National Park, Spain.

ECOSYSTEM

The ecosystem is an area containing living organisms interacting with each other, including the water, the sun, and the air. They work together in an area known as a unit, which can be simply a bubble of water or miles of a desert. Each is unique and has established balance through time, which is an important part of all life forms.

Aerial shot of the Great Barrier Reef.

BIOME

This describes a larger group of comparable ecosystems. They each will be consisting of similar plants, animals, rainfall, and weather. There are many biomes on Earth. Some examples of biomes are grasslands, desert, tundra, savanna, tundra, tropical rainforest, temperate forest, and taiga forest. Examples of aquatic biomes include marine, freshwater, and coral reefs.

Australia sunrise.

MARINE BIOMES

The two major aquatic biomes are the marine and freshwater biomes. The marine biome consists primarily of saltwater oceans. This is the largest biome on Earth and this planet is covered by about 70% of saltwater oceans.

Even though a marine biome is made primarily of our oceans, there are three different types:

OCEANS – There are basically five oceans that cover the planet, including the Southern, Artic, Indian, Pacific, and Atlantic.

CORAL REEFS - Coral reefs are smaller than oceans, but approximately 25% of marine species live in these reefs making them a vital biome.

Coral and fish in the Red Sea. Egypt, Africa.

ESTUARIES - These are areas where streams and rivers flow into our oceans. This then creates an ecosystem or biome with fascinating and distinct animal and plant life.

Brook.

Pacific Ocean Coast California.

OCEAN LIGHT ZONES

The ocean can then be separated in three zones or layers. These are known as light zones due to the amount of sunlight that is received in each layer.

Ocean Zones.

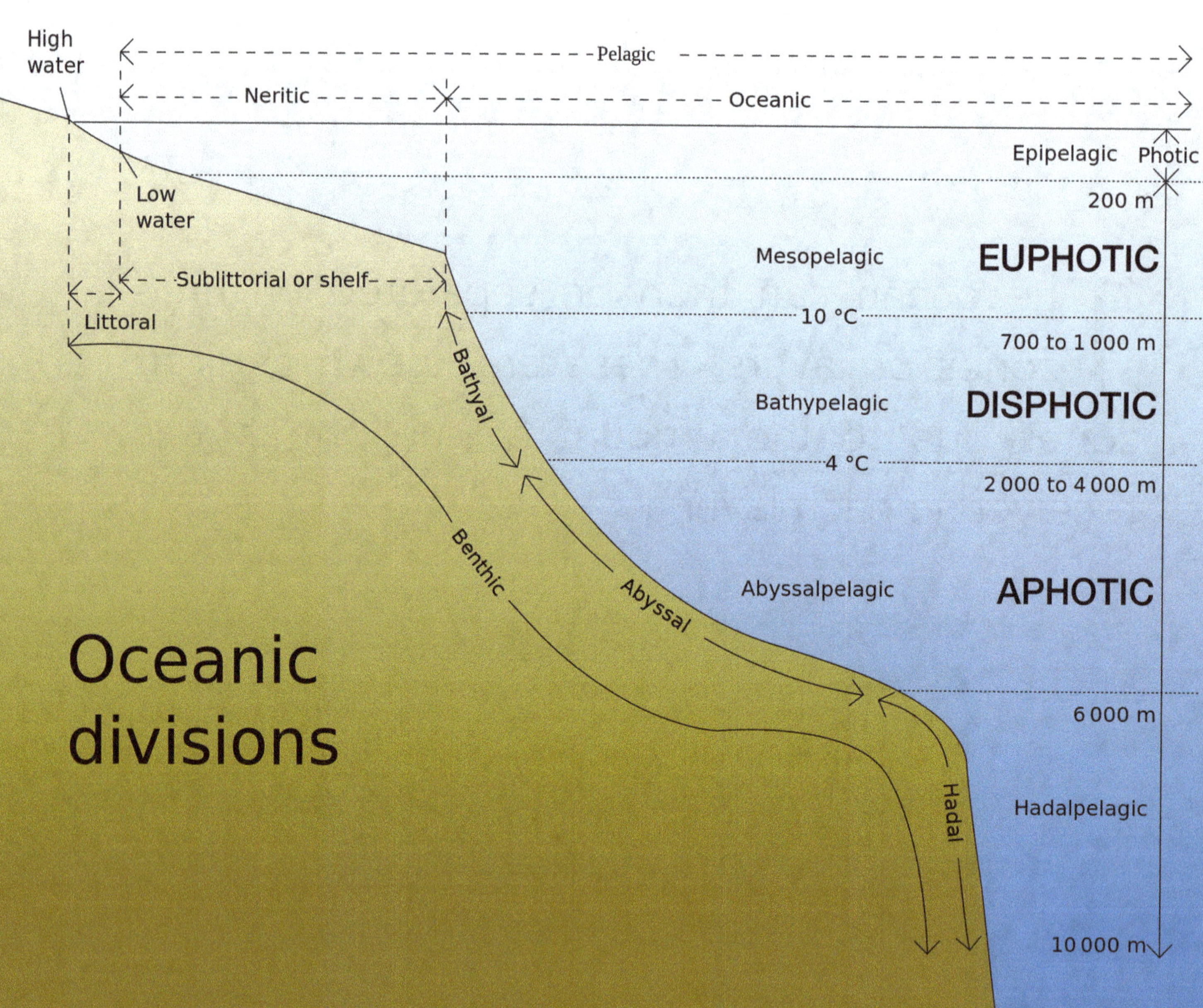

High
water
Pelagic
Neritic
Oceanic
Low
water
Epipelagic
Photic
200 m
Mesopelagic
EUPHOTIC
Sublittorial or shelf
10 °C
700 to 1 000 m
Littoral
Bathyal
Bathypelagic
DISPHOTIC
4 °C
2 000 to 4 000 m
Benthic
Abyssal
Abyssalpelagic
APHOTIC
Oceanic
divisions
6 000 m
Hadal
Hadalpelagic
10 000 m

THE SUNLIT (EUPHOTIC ZONE) is the topmost layer of the ocean and because of this, it receives the greatest amount of sunlight. While its depth fluctuates, it averages about 600 feet deep. Photosynthesis is the process where this sunlight provides energy to the organisms in the ocean. It provides food for plants as well as the plankton, which are very tiny organisms in the ocean. Plankton play a very important role in the ocean since they supply food for much of the remaining ocean life. Because of this, approximately 90% of the ocean life is located in the euphotic zone (sunlit zone).

THE TWILIGHT (DISPHOTIC ZONE) is known as the middle zone of the ocean. It ranges from approximately 600 feet to approximately 3,000 feet deep, dependent upon how clear or murky the water might be. There is not enough sunlight for the plants to live in this zone. Any animals that are able to live here have become accustomed to surviving with a small amount of light. Many of these animals are able to produce light themselves using bioluminescence, which is created through chemical reaction.

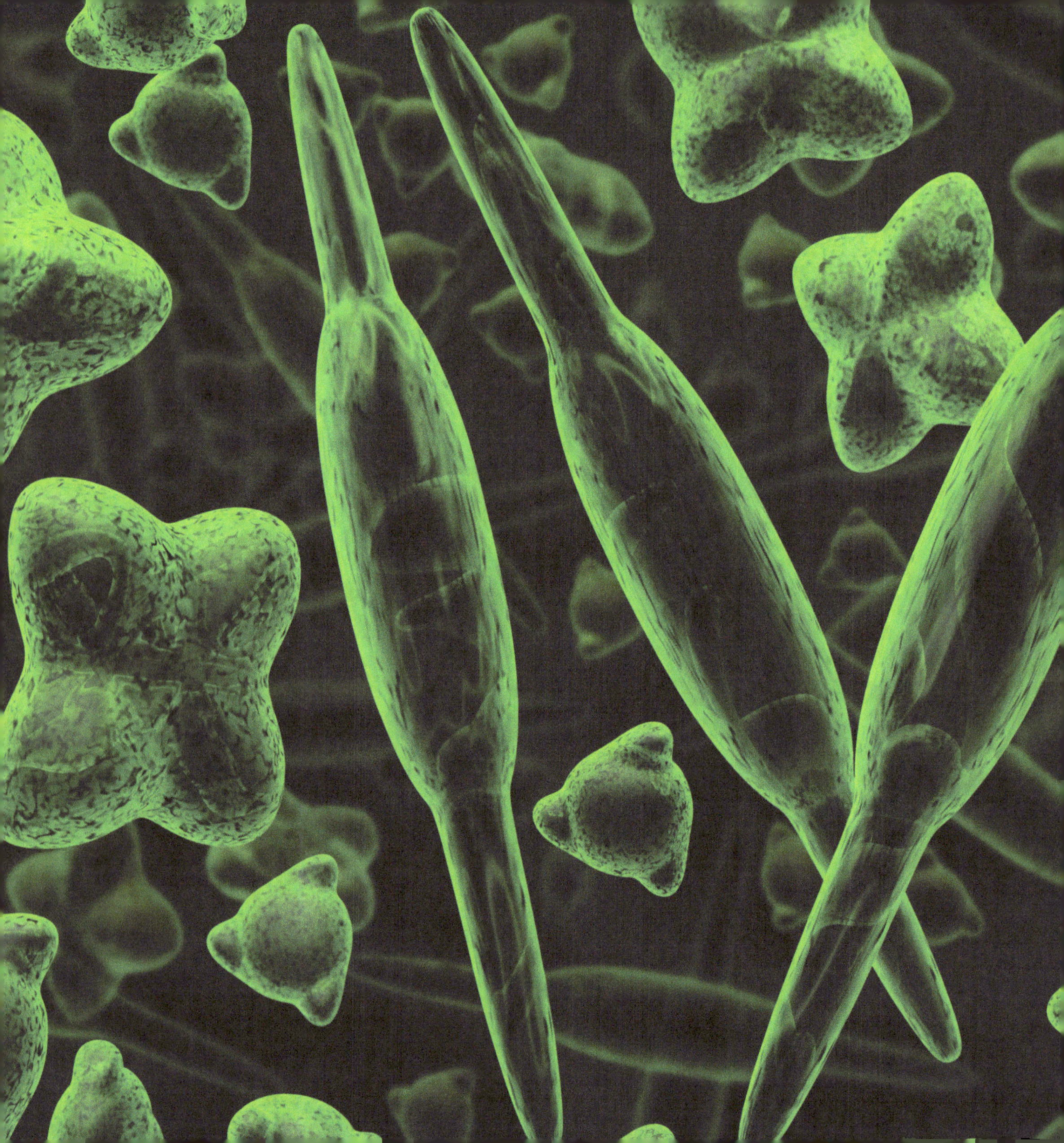

THE MIDNIGHT (APHOTIC ZONE) is below 3,000 feet and it is completely dark. It is extremely cold and its water pressure is very high. Very few animals are able to exist under these conditions. Only a few animals have adapted to live in these extreme conditions. Any that can survive, live from the bacteria which obtains it energy from the cracks that form in the Earth located at the ocean bottom. Approximately 90% of our ocean is in the midnight zone.

A school of fish swimming.

ANIMALS LIVING IN THE MARINE BIOME

The marine biome contains the most biodiverse animals off all biomes. Many animals, including fish, have gills, allowing them to breathe the water. Other ones are considered mammals and they have to rise to the surface of the ocean to breath, but can still spend a greater part of their life underwater. We will be discussing more about some of these animals on the following pages.

FISH – Grouper, Sharks, Gars, Swordfish, Clown Fish, Stringer, Flatfish, Rockfish, Eels, Sunfish Mola, Seahorse and Tuna.

MARINE MAMMALS – Manatees, Blue Whales, Otters, Seals, Manatees, Walruses and Dolphins.

Humpback whale.

MOLLUSKS – Clams, Octopus, Cuttlefish, Clams, Conch, Squids, Oysters, Slugs and Snails.

PLANTS LIVING IN THE MARINE BIOME

There are thousands of different plant species living in our oceans. They survive by relying on photosynthesis providing energy from the sun. Plant survival in the ocean is extremely significant for life on our great planet Earth. The algae in the ocean absorbs the carbon dioxide and is then able to provide oxygen to the Earth. Phytoplankton and kelp are examples of algae. Some of the other plants of the ocean are mangroves, sea grasses, and seaweed.

Closeup colorful coral.

Kinney Lake.

FRESHWATER

The freshwater biome contains a low salt content as compared to the marine biome which consists of saltwater.

FRESHWATER BIOMES

Freshwater Biomes consist mainly of wetlands, streams and rivers, ponds and lakes.

PONDS AND LAKES

Ponds and lakes are also referred to as lentic ecosystems and have standing or still waters, and they do not move like streams and rivers.

Lakes are frequently separated into four zones of biotic groups similar to the zones in the oceans:

LITTORAL ZONE - This is the area that is closest to the shore where aquatic plants are able to grow.

LIMNETIC ZONE - This is the open surface of the waters of a lake, away from its shore.

EUPHOTIC ZONE - This is the area below its surface and is still able to obtain sunlight for the photosynthesis process.

BENTHIC ZONE - This is the bottom, or floor, of the lake.

Over time, temperatures in the lakes can change. Lakes in tropical areas will maintain the same relative temperature and as you go deeper into the water, the colder it will become. In the northern lakes, the temperatures will change in accordance with the seasons.

LAKE ANIMALS – Includes fish, plankton, snails, crayfish, worms, turtles, frogs, and insects.

LAKE PLANTS - Includes bladderwort, water lilies, cattail, stonewort, bulrush, and duckweed.

STREAMS AND RIVERS

Streams and Rivers are also referred to as lotic ecosystems and they have waters that flow, unlike the waters that remain still in lakes and ponds. They vary in size.

Rivers and streams are often called lotic ecosystems. This means that they have flowing waters, unlike the still waters of ponds and lakes. This biome varies substantially in size from a small trickling stream to rivers that might travel for over a thousand miles and be over a mile wide.

Beautiful waterfall in forest.

Key factors that influence their ecology are:

FLOW – The strength that it flows and the amount of water impacts the species of animals and plants that are able to survive in a river.

LIGHT – Light provides the energy for plants through photosynthesis. Factors such as the amount of light available due to seasonal changes will affect the river's ecosystem since light is necessary for photosynthesis.

TEMPERATURE - The weather of the land through which a river flows will also impact local animal and plant life.

CHEMISTRY – This refers to type of geology through which the river is flowing. It impacts what type of soil, rocks, and nutrients are in the river.

RIVER ANIMALS - Live in or near the river and includes crabs, snails, and insects; fish such as salmon and catfish; and beavers, otters, crocodiles, snakes, and salamanders.

RIVER PLANTS - Grow around the rivers and vary quite a bit dependent upon where the river is located. These plants will typically live along the edge of a river where the water is moving slower. Plants include river birch, water stargrass, tapegrass, and willow trees.

Marshy ecological reserve is a gathering spot for various birds in winter.

WETLANDS BIOME

The wetlands biome made of a combination of water and land. Think of it as an area of land saturated with water. It might be land that is mostly underwater during a certain time of year or flooded only at certain times. One of its significant characteristics is the ability to support aquatic plant life.

Wetlands include marshes, swamps, and bogs. They are often found close to larger bodies of water like river and lakes and are located all over the world.

They can also play an important role with nature. They prevent flooding when they are located near rivers. They also play a role in purifying and filtering the water. The wetlands are also home to a wide variety of animals and plants.

WETLAND ANIMALS - Wetlands provide a home for a vast diversity in animal life. Reptiles, birds, and amphibians all survive well in the wetlands. The crocodiles and alligators are its largest predators. Other animals that are able to survive in the wetlands include deer, racoons, minks, and beavers.

WETLAND PLANTS - Wetland plants have the ability to float on top of the water or grow entirely underwater. Other plants, like large trees, live mostly out of the water. Some of the plants include mangroves, cypress trees, cattail, duckweed, water lilies, and milkweed.

Now that you have learned about the fresh and saltwater ecosystems, you can search the internet or go to your local library for additional information, as well as asking questions of your teachers, family, and friends.

Visit
BABY PROFESSOR
EDUCATION KIDS
www.BabyProfessorBooks.com
to download Free Baby Professor eBooks
and view our catalog of new and exciting
Children's Books